Disgusting Poems

BBBurp!!

Compiled by

Paul Cookson

Illustrated by

Sarah Nayler

■SCHOLASTIC

Dedicated to Eric, Heather, Alice and Aiden.
With thanks to Orston and Rosedale
Primary Schools.

Scholastic Children's Books,
Euston House, 24 Eversholt Street,
London, NW1 1DB, UK
a division of Scholastic Ltd
London ~ New York ~ Toronto ~ Sydney ~ Auckland
Mexico City ~ New Delhi ~ Hong Kong

Published in the UK by Scholastic Ltd, 2004
This collection copyright © Paul Cookson, 2004
Illustrations copyright © Sarah Nayler, 2004

Copyright information for individual poems is given on page 126, which
constitutes an extension of this copyright page.

10 digit ISBN 0 439 96880 1
13 digit ISBN 978 0439 96880 5

Printed and bound by Nørhaven Paperback AS, Denmark

4 6 8 10 9 7 5 3

CONTENTS

First Word

Whose Verse is it Anyway?

My teacher gave me a book.
"You might enjoy this," she said.
I gave it a glance.
It was a book of poems
But the cover was cool.
Then I looked at the title:
"Disgusting Poems".
"Yeah, right," I thought
"Love and Daffodils and all that.
Too true – disgusting!"
Then I opened it.
Then I read one.
I read another one…
They were all about sick
And spots and lavatories…
Then I really *was* disgusted.
I put it back.
What's left for us
To share and hide and giggle at
When grown ups
Start giving us books like that?

Trevor Millum

Animal Instincts

Our Dog

Our dog, Mick,
Is a mucky pup.
He's just been sick,
And he's licked it up!

John Kitching

Question: What wild and fearsome animal goes

W
E
E
E
E
E
E
E
E
E
E
E
E
E
E
E
E

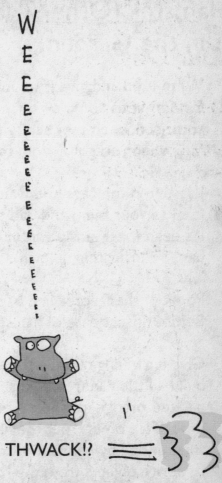

THWACK!?

Answer: A bungee-jumping hippo
after a particularly heavy snack.

Barry Buckingham

Ten Things to do with a Dead Hamster (Other Than Burying it in the Garden)

1. Wrap it up and give it to your brother/sister for Christmas or their birthday, look surprised when they scream, and say it was fine when you got it from the shop.

2. Leave it in the cage and wait to see how long it takes your mum and dad to work out that it's dead (best in the winter, unless you always have your heating up high).

3. Pop it in the freezer in a bag marked: Best Before (insert date of hamster's demise).

4. Give it a Viking burial – the full monty, i.e., build a little Viking ship, stick on bits of painted orange cardboard to make it look as though it's on fire, put the hamster in it, surrounded by hamster food-treats and favourite objects from the hamster's life. Fill the bath, and launch the little ship on the water. Leave it there for your mum to discover when she goes to run that long, relaxing bath she likes.

5. Have it stuffed and mounted and keep it on your desk.

6. Have it stuffed and mounted and give it to your granny for Christmas.

7. Have it stuffed and mounted and use it as a door stop.

8. Donate its little body to veterinary science.

9. Have it stuffed and use it in a playground game of catch, rounders, football, etc.

10. Take it back to the shop where you got it, weep, complain bitterly, and ask for your money back or a new hamster.

Tony Bradman

Head Lice

Head lice are not nice –
you don't know you got 'em,
it's quite hard to spot 'em –
but they're terribly catching,
and soon you'll be hatching
a head full and scratching.
Before you're aware
there's a colony there,
all sucking your blood
through your scalp in your hair.
You comb out with tea-tree
for hours till they're banished,
and worry for weeks with
each itch they're not vanished –
whilst watching your friends'
eyes to check for a cringe,
when they spot a stray head louse
peer out through your fringe.
Head lice are not nice,
you don't know you got 'em,
they're terribly catching,
it's quite hard to spot 'em,
could be millions there in
your hair for dispatching,
so before they're installed
and before you start scratching,

before they've infested
and nested and crawled,
save yourself now,
and shave yourself bald!

Liz Brownlee

The Dung Beetle's Song

We'd be eating crusty pizza,
were we clever like you people,
but we're small and not too smart,
we're a little, bug-brained beetle,
and we eat dung!

Could've fancied figs or fish cakes,
fruit-filled flans or scrambled eggs,
apple pies or Danish pastries,
Swedish meat balls, French frogs' legs,
but we chose dung.

Cows and sheep eat grass and clover,
every horse must have its hay,
pandas binge on bamboo shoots,
while all the live-long day
we devour dung.

You've got chip shops, you've got cafés,
you've got ritzy restaurants,
sit-down bars and hot dog stands,
but all we seem to want's
somewhere serving dung!

And the moment we are able,
it might even be from birth,
while you're making for McDonald's,
we're out scouring the earth
for a diet of dung.

Please don't misunderstand me,
don't think me simply crude,
but if the world were sensible,
when we pooed we would poo food.
'Cause we eat dung.

While you breakfast on your Bran Flakes,
or take buttered toast for tea,
even sip some soup for supper,
won't you spare a thought for me –
dining out on dung.

But what if I'm a numbskull? What if I am a nitwit?
Bug that I am, I'm man enough to stand here and
        admit it –
I was *wrung*!

We'd be eating crusty pizza,
were we clever like you people,
but we're small and not too smart,
we're a little bug-brained beetle,
and we eat dung!

David Horner

Gran's Dog

Gran's dog is disgusting.
He's always shedding hairs.
He sheds them on the carpets.
He sheds them on the stairs.

He jumps up on your lap
And slobbers on your knees,
Then lifts his leg to scratch himself.
I'm sure that he's got fleas.

He's always doing silent ones
That smell of rotten eggs.
He seizes every chance he gets
To sniff between *your* legs.

When he does his business,
Gran says, "You're a clever pup."
Then hands me the pooper-scoop
And I have to clear it up.

His breath is foul and fetid,
When he gives your face a lick.
Gran's dog is disgusting.
He really makes me sick!

John Foster

Growth or Moan

"*She who stands in cowpat grows*"
is how the age-old saying goes

so being tiny, too petite,
I slipped the shoes from off my feet
and shed the socks that warmed my toes
then poised in ballerina pose
to ...
overbalance!
with a thrust
one foot broke through the cowpat crust
and pure manure of mustard hue
adorned where once I'd worn a shoe
whilst waves of warmth swept ankle high,
and splattered splots festooned my eye

and even if I'd be believed
I can't tell what my mouth received
because that orifice is blocked
(with powers of speech severely shocked).

That age-old saying should, methinks,
be, "*She who stands in cowpat stinks*".

Gina Douthwaite

Deep Pile

In town –
The weekend shopping trip.
My foot –
A horrid squelchy slip!
Examine shoe
And curse my luck –
I've trodden in
A pile of muck!
And all its
Pale brown oozy goo
Is plastered on
My dark brown shoe.
Well don't just stand there
Looking down,
Admiring different
Shades of brown:
Do something!
Other shoppers stare.
So wipe it off!
OK but where?
No clump of grass
To scrub my clog
Clean of that
Disgusting dog.

But wait – a carpet shop
Door wide!
Gingerly
I step inside,
Eyes darting
Every which direction,
Looking for the
Deep Pile Section.

Eric Finney

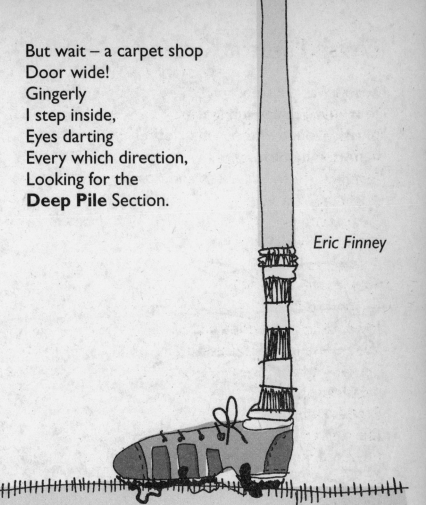

I Wish I was a Kitten

I wish I was a kitten,
life would be such fun.
I'd frisk around without my clothes
then sit and lick my

       ...ears and nose.

Jane Clarke

Knickers and Pants

Nickie's Knickers

Nickie's knickers are fantastic:
sparkly, silky, scarlet plastic —
perfect for her acts gymnastic
but for the absence of elastic.

Kate Williams

How Long Have You Worn Those Pants?

How long have you worn that shirt?
It's stained from ketchup, crisps and Coke, and six
     types of dessert.
You could boil it up for soup, and feed an army,
     it's a cert,
From the slops and spills and splashes on that
     shirt.

How long have you worn those socks?
They smell like something putrid that's been
     fished out of the docks.
If you catch bubonic plague, or some such
     pestilence or pox,
It'll be because you didn't change those socks!

How long have you worn that vest?
On second thoughts, don't let me know; I'll only
     get depressed.
But I'd rather delve in droppings from a long-
     dead dodo's nest,
Than come anywhere near that vest!

How long have you worn those pants?

("*The rest of this verse has been censored. It's too disgusting even for me.*" Editor)

Paul Bright

My Week was Pants

Mum bought me a pack of patterned pants
And I'm very sad she got them
As all this week I've been to school
With strange things across my bottom

Monday's pants had little yachts sailing on the seas;
Tuesday's pants had butterflies and fuzzy buzzy bees;
Wednesday's pants had teddies dancing by in lines;
Thursday's pants had roses, hearts and valentines;
But Friday's pants made me ashamed to even
show my face;
Frothy ballerinas in tutus trimmed with lace.

On Saturday and Sunday, I didn't go to school;
I stayed at home all weekend and wore no pants
    at all.

John Coldwell

Grandad's Pants

Grandad's pants billow on the washing line
Like the enormous sails of an old ship,
Ready to voyage to a distant land –
Maybe they'll sail to the West Undies.

Coral Rumble

Gran's Big Bloomers

In Gran's big bloomers
You could hide...

An air balloon
For her to ride;
A baby hippo
(Small but wide);
A roundabout,
A swing, a slide;
A string of flags
All brightly dyed;
A stack of pancakes
Crisply fried;
A pair of llamas
(Both cross-eyed);
A princess,
Shocked yet dignified;
A whale or wombat —
(You decide);
A bridegroom and
His blushing bride;
A queue of tourists,
Plus their guide;
A plague of rats
With Piper (Pied);
A giant parcel
Neatly tied...

And STILL have room
For Gran inside.

Clare Bevan

29

A Disgusting Poem

Sir said: write a disgusting poem
about embarrassing stuff –
spots and sick and toilets
and belly-button fluff…

And I thought: "That's enough!"

I like poems
    about the songs
        my mother sometimes sings

and the moon
    and the stars
        on a summer night

and lying in bed
    on Sunday when
        the church bell rings

and the glint of creamy white
    on waves on foreign shores
        and the delicate

marmalade-coloured fur
    on my kitten's paws,
        and starlings' purple wings…

So I wrote that

    and Sir said: Fred,
you haven't done what I said.
Forget the moon and the stars at night
write about knickers instead.

Fred Sedgwick

Bellies, Bottoms and Body Bits

Pretty Parents

Dad's got tattoos on his chest,
But he's not as bad as Mum.
She's the most embarrassing –
She's got tattoos on her bum!

Clive Webster

Bottom

Who'd be a bottom? Not me.

Always facing the wrong way.
To go for a walk
And not be able to see
Where you are going.

To be sat upon all day.
Smacked. Called rude names.
Whistled at. Laughed at.
The butt of a hundred jokes.

Faithful to the end.
An undercover agent
Working all hours
And getting no thanks for it.

Alas, poor bottom.

Roger McGough

The Day I Got my Finger Stuck up my Nose

When I got my finger stuck up my nose
I went to a doctor, who said,
"Nothing like this has happened before,
We will have to chop off your head."

"It's only my finger stuck up my nose,
It's only my finger!" I said.
"I can see what it is," the doctor replied,
"But we'll still have to chop off your head."

He went to the cabinet. He took out an axe.
I watched with considerable dread.
"But it's only my finger stuck up my nose.
It's only a finger!" I said.

"Perhaps we can yank it out with a hook
Tied to some surgical thread.
Maybe we can try that," he replied,
"Rather than chop off your head."

"I'm never going to pick it again.
I've now learned my lesson," I said.
"I won't stick my finger up my nose –
I'll stick it in my ear instead."

Brian Patten

34

Snug as a Bug

I am your belly-button bug.
My home with you is warm and snug.
Of course, there isn't only me:
I'm speaking for the family
(At the last count forty three),
Expressing keen appreciation
Of our rent-free situation
Nestled within your navel fluff
And other slightly manky stuff.
Are we crowded? Not at all,
We button bugs are very small.
Nourishment, of course, we get
From your abundant belly sweat
And passing germs are tasty fare –
We catch them off your underwear.
You do give us an anxious hour
When you take your annual shower
But huddled down against the spray
We haven't yet been washed away.
Apart from that, we have no fears –
We haven't been disturbed for years.
So thanks again from forty three
For your kind hospitality.

Eric Finney

Art Museum

"Please, don't touch!
Please, no noise!
Pay attention,
girls and boys!"

"Please, don't yawn!
Please, don't sit!
Chewing gum
we don't permit!"

They've dragged us on a field trip to
this musty old museum.
We're lookin' at some paintings now,
but I don't wanna see 'em.

We have to "*stay together*" and "*be quiet*"–
that's "*the rule*".
I thought I'd never say this, but
I'd rather be in school.

Wait a second … Holy smokes!
It's getting better now!
If you could see what I am seeing,
all you'd say is … "WOW!"

Museums are amazing,
as anybody knows.
'Cause people in some paintings,
(and on a bunch of statues, too)

AREN'T WEARING ANY CLOTHES!

Ted Scheu

Tush, Tush!

Let's pretend today
that *bottom*
is a rude word.

Write a list of
alternative words,
like *behind*,
backside,
and *sit-upon*.

The one with
the longest list
will be given
a packet of
wine bums.

John C. Desmond

Bite at a Blister

Bite at a blister,
tug with your teeth,
get at the gunge
bubbling beneath.

Gobble it down,
leaving no waste,
for the bigger the blister
the better the taste!

Andrew Collett

Bad Habits

Party Trick

Pick a bogey from your nose
Then roll it on your tongue.
An easy trick for good old Dad –
His tongue's six inches long.

Clive Webster

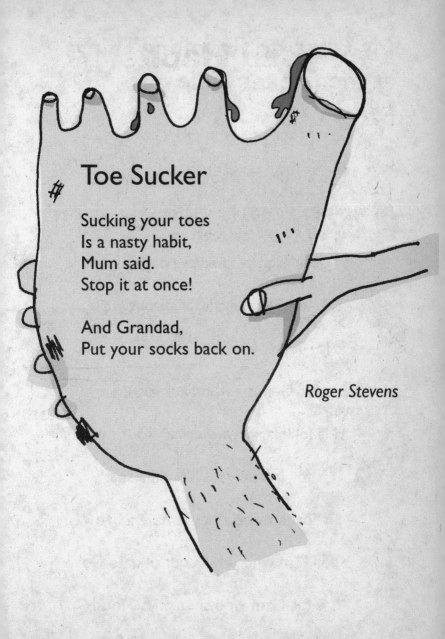

Toe Sucker

Sucking your toes
Is a nasty habit,
Mum said.
Stop it at once!

And Grandad,
Put your socks back on.

Roger Stevens

My Class do Revolting Things at the Dinner Table

 A is for Anna who picks her nose

B is for Bruce who picks his toenails

 C is for Claire who eats maggot pie

D is for Dan who drinks bogey brew

 E is for Ellen who eats sprout stew

F is for Frank who eats worms on toast

 G is for Gemma who likes rotten eggs

H is for Harry who drinks sour milk

 I is for Ireane who lets off a smell

J is for Jim who doesn't have a bath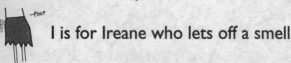

 K is for Kim who drinks out of date Coke

L is for Liam who spits on his food

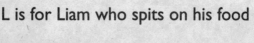 M is for Mandy who likes to eat liver

N is for Niall who brings frogs' legs

O is for Olivia who drinks snail slime

P is for Peter who licks earwax

Q is for Quinter who eats mouldy apples

R is for Rosie who licks salsa dip

S is for Sam who eats raw parsnips

T is for Tom who drinks snot juice

U is for Una who eats chickens' eyes

V is for Victor who eats with his hands

W is for Wendy who's mad on roast cockroach

X is for Xena who eats head-lice stew

Y is for Yorick who drinks vinegar

Z is for Zac ... well, let's not talk about Zac.

Scott Richards (aged 10)

Champion of the School

I'm the loudest burping, armpit honking
Top paper plane making
Best funny face pulling
Double jointed knuckle crackling
Most consistent homework losing
Most inventive earwax moulding
Highest number chip chewing
Biggest bubblegum blowing
Smelliest sweaty sock sniffing
Furthest paper pellet throwing
Most finger nose picking
Long distance bogey flicking
Raspberry blowing, tongue sticking
Ear clipping, bottom kicking
Pimple popping, zit splitting
Wall hitting slick spitting
Sneezing, wheezing, toe cheesing
Thunderpanted loud chanted
Champion Of The School!

Signed,
Miss B. A. Ving
(Reception Teacher)

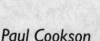

Paul Cookson

There was an Old Man from Darjeeling

There was an old man from Darjeeling,
Who boarded a bus bound for Ealing.
    He saw on the door:
    "Please don't spit on the floor",
So he stood up and spat on the ceiling.

Anon

Oo-Phew!
(Or what can happen to dirty boys)

Arnie wouldn't brush his teeth
Or comb his hair
Or spray his feet.

He wouldn't shower after Games
Or take a bath
Or trim his nails.

He wouldn't wipe his fluey nose
Or mucky chin
Or yucky toes.

He never scrubbed his scabby knees
His belly button
Smelt like cheese.

His ears were full of gungy wax
And as for zits – well
He had stacks.

One sweltering, hot summer's day
Arnie felt tired
So down he lay.

And as he lay his body sweated
Whiffs so strong
That they were gaseous.

He exploded with a yell
In one **horrendous**
Awful SMELL!

Patricia Leighton

Shut Your Mouth When You're Eating

Shut your mouth when you're eating.
    I am, Dad.
MOUTH!
    It *is* shut.
I can see it isn't. I can *hear* it isn't.
    What about *his* mouth? You can see
everything in his mouth.
He's only two. He doesn't know any better.
    You can see all his peas and tomato sauce.
That's none of your business.

(2 MINUTES GO BY)

Dad.
Yes.
    Your mouth's open. Shut your mouth when
        you're eating.
It is shut, thank you very much.
    I can see it isn't, Dad. I can see all the food
        in there.
Look that's my business, OK?
    Peas, gravy, spuds, everything.
Look, you don't want to grow up to be as
    horrible as your father
do you? Answer that, smartyboots.

Michael Rosen

Dear Teacher

Please don't stress but I have something to
    confess.
I'm about to let slip the truth of our school
    camping trip.

You wiped out all our smiles, making us hike for
    twenty miles.
And when we fell to the floor, you forced us up
    to do five more.

Do you recall that taste in your mouth when,
    next morning, we marched south?
Well I've always kept this hush: for revenge
    I nicked your toothbrush and
for a solid hour I suppose (or who knows!),
    I used it to clean between my toes.

Sorry

Ian Corns

Ian Corns

Underneath Dad's Armchair

Underneath Dad's armchair
where the vacuum never goes,
you'll find fingernail scrapings
and gremlins from his nose.

You'll find tissues stuck together
and biscuits with green skin,
you'll find waving bits of toenail
and whiskers from his chin.

You'll find dried-up spots and pimples
and pickings from his teeth,
you'll find earwax and tummy fluff
all lurking down beneath.

For under our dad's armchair,
there before your eyes
you'll find a foul and filthy world
which grows each day in size.

Andrew Collett

Spots, Sick and Toilet Troubles

Sick

Eating curry
in a hurry
made me want to v**O**mit.

Ate it slowly
second time
with some pickle on it.

Gina Douthwaite

Lucinda's Sick in the Sink

Lucinda's sick in the sink
Lucinda's sick in the sink
It's green and yellow and pink
Lucinda's sick in the sink

Bits of carrot, bits of cheese,
Bits of sweetcorn, bits of peas,
Bits that look like someone's sneeze

Lucinda's sick in the sink
Lucinda's sick in the sink
That sickly stinky stink
Lucinda's sick in the sink

Lots of liquid, lots of lumps,
Lots and lots of greasy chunks
Lots of gastronomic gunk

Lucinda's sick in the sink
Lucinda's sick in the sink
It's much worse than you think
Lucinda's sick in the sink

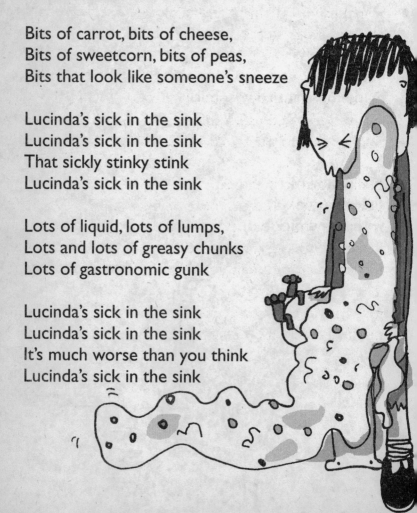

Splattered walls, splattered door,
Splattered table, splattered floor,
Spattered scattered splattered more

Lucinda's sick in the sink
Lucinda's sick in the sink
It makes you grimace and blink
Lucinda's sick in the sink

Teachers try to use the mop
Paper towels, paper cups
But it never seems to stop
She just keeps on chucking up…

Lucinda's sick in the sink
Lucinda's sick in the sink
It makes your nostrils shrink
It makes you grimace and blink
It's much worse than you think
That sickly stinky stink
Green and yellow and pink
Lucinda's sick in the sink
Bleurgh!

Paul Cookson

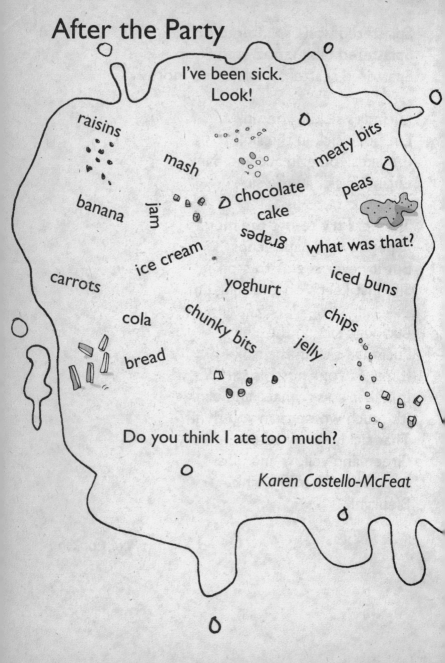

After the Party

I've been sick.
Look!

raisins

mash

meaty bits

banana

jam

chocolate
cake

peas

grapes

what was that?

ice cream

carrots

yoghurt

iced buns

cola

chunky bits

chips

bread

jelly

Do you think I ate too much?

Karen Costello-McFeat

Disgusting Books to Read on the Loo

All About Bottoms by Lou Paper

On the Run by Di Arear

Dirty Nappy by P. Dan Pooed

NOSTRILS – THE INSIDE STORY BY A. BOGEY

About To Throw Up by I. Feelsick

Body Odours by R. M. Pitts

A Snotty Nose by U. R. Smellie

THE SEWER RAT'S STORY BY O. WOTAPONG

Overflowing Urinals by P. Everywhere

Ivor Cheek

Breakfast

It isn't really a good idea
To eat burger and chocs in the car
As they're sure to reappear once more
Before you've gone too far.
Your stomach will start to rumble
Your face will start to turn green
And Booaaaaagghffff there goes your breakfast
Across the A19.

Gareth Owen

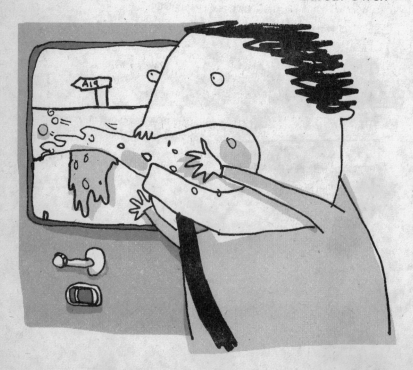

Diary of a Toilet Seat

Today's been an up and down kind of day
A girl then boy kind of day
A sunny and showers kind of day
Not a sit down on the job kind of day
BUTT a stand up – sit down kind of day
A meeting up with old friends kind of day
And a lot of new faces kind of day.

I hope tonight is a lie down and sleep kind
   of day
BUTT I bet it will be another
Stand up and guard the tank kind of night.

No BUTTS they say … no BUTTS
If only that were true.

Daniel Phelps

Advice to Anyone Cooped Up in a Hot Car on a Long Journey

Never let your thoughts stray
Away from the beauty of the day.
Under the glories of the blue
Sky are the splendours of the new view:
Earth's pleasures in every direction
Are laid out now for your inspection.

And remember to keep
Normal breathing
Deep, deep, deep, deep, deep.

Valiant traveller on this long, long road
Overcome your demons with this advice code
Maintain your grip on the main trick
If you want to avoid being travel s_ _k
Try not to read this acrostic.

John Clarke

58

Babies Don't Care

What's your baby brother doing?
Why's he gone all red?
Why's he screwing up his face
And shaking his bald head?
Why's he wriggling like that –
All squirmy in his seat?
And why's he stretching out his legs
From his hips down to his feet?
Oh, he looks OK now
He's grinning. Seems quite happy.

Happy? He's ecstatic…
He's just filled up his nappy.

Jan Dean

The Day I Fell Down the Toilet

The day I fell down the toilet
Is a day I'll never forget,
One moment I was in comfort
The next I was helpless and wet.

My feet tipped up to the ceiling
My body collapsed in the bowl,
In haste I grabbed at the handle
And found myself flushed down a hole

One wave goodbye to the bathroom
And I was lost in the sewer,
Travelling tunnels and caverns
On a raft made out of manure.

Then came the washing-up water
With bits of spaghetti and peas,
The filth from a local factory
And an undiscovered disease.

Drifting along in the darkness,
There was nothing to do but wait.
What would I say to my mum now?
What was it that made me so late?

Suddenly it was all over,
From the end of a pipe I shot
Into a part of the ocean
Where the rubbish was sent to rot.

Glad to escape from the tunnel
To leave all pollution behind,
I found a nice spot on the beach
Then started to bathe and unwind.

But bad things began to pursue me
They stuck to my feet and my hand,
Wreckage was surfing the wave tops
And oil lay around on the sand.

I figured the sewer was safer
For no one said sewers were clean,
I found the pipe that I came from.
And waded my way back upstream.

When I got home I was shattered,
I was filthy, ragged and wet,
Rattling the bathroom door was Dad
Saying, "You off that toilet yet?"

Steve Turner

Pimple Potion Number Nine

Do you seek a simple pimple
or a double-dimpled wart,
with one long hair, in the middle,
maybe several – black and short?
I've a notion that this potion
can bring spots or zits in zillions
plus battalions of verrucas
(snooker-ball-sized, bright vermilion).
Blackheads, bunions, boils, big freckles,
choice carbuncles, crusty corns…
Shake the bottle: check the dosage;
give to victims, night and morn.
Guaranteed to be effective,
yes, I can safely say,
not an ocean of blotch lotion
could wash the splotch away.
Try some! Buy some! You'll be fine –
Pimple Potion Number Nine.

Mike Johnson

Rude Food and Rotten Recipes

Little Jack Horner

Little Jack Horner
Sat in a corner
Eating a ham and egg pie
He pulled out a sliver
Of some mouse's liver
And most of the same mouse's eye.

David Kitchen

The Last Recorder No One Wants to Play

It's dirty and manky, grubby and smelly,
Not cleaned out for several years.
It's been up a thousand noses
And in twice as many ears.

Greasy, grimy, slippy, slimy,
Dried up phlegm that looks like cheese
Dribble from a thousand spitters
A breeding ground for all disease.

Bubblegum, tops from cold sores,
Bogeys, earwax, mixed with chips
crisps and crumbs and bits of filling,
Gravy blobs and apple pips.

So … late arrivals to Recorders
Always make Miss Morgan's day
Smiling she gives out the last one
No one ever wants to play.

Miss Morgan smiles with satisfaction
Revenge is sweet and hers alone
And if you think that it's disgusting …
Look inside the last trombone!

Paul Cookson

Food (and what's in it and what's done to it that makes it so disgusting)

Pota**toes**
Pears
Gr**apes**
Boiled eggs
Marm**a**lade
Chips
Crum**pets**
Mu**ffins**
Rib **eye** steak
Chewing **gums**
Fish **fingers**
Tongue
Liver (and onions)!
Leg of lamb
Shoulder of pork
Jelly **babies**
Battered cod
Egg – first beaten
then left strangled at the bottom of the pan.

Lisa Watkinson

Going One Better

Sister ate a spoonful of soil
So I chewed a worm

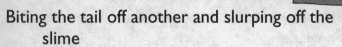

She ate half a worm
So I had two whole slugs

Biting the tail off another and slurping off the
    slime
she sucked four snails out of their shells in one
    go.

Not to be outdone I made a frogspawn sandwich
(with last week's bread) … and bit into it …
    twice.

She snatched it away, added three caterpillars,
a handful of ants and carried on munching.

I went and took a great big gulp from the dog's
    water bowl

She went and took a great big mouthful of dog
    food.

I told her that rabbit droppings were raisins …

So she got a shovel full and gobbled them all up.

I was just about to mash up a cowpat into a stew
when Dad came outside and shouted us in for tea.

'What's for tea?" we said.
"Liver and cabbage!" said Dad.

"Yeeeuuuchhh!" we both shouted
"Now that's what I call really disgusting."

Paul Cookson

Accidents at Teatime

I gave my Uncle Ronnie
a cup of tea I'd sneezed in
he didn't seem to notice
in fact, it seemed to please him.

I gave my Auntie Lynda
a scrummy slice of cake
but a bit of coughed out spit
dropped on it by mistake.

I gave my cousin Simon
a sandwich made of chicken
that I noticed far too late
the cat had just been sick in.

The pie I gave my sister
had an appetizing smell
but the plaster from my finger
had dropped in there as well.

I passed a plate of ice cream
to my hungry mum
who didn't see the lumpy bits
were chewed up bubblegum.

They shouted and were angry
I worried not a jot
because I saw them drink the milk
in which I'd popped my spot.

David Harmer

Mr O'Donnell's Parents' Evening Plan

Overworked, underpaid and tired,
very, very tired,
Mr O'Donnell prepares for parents' evening

He will have a snack of
garlic bread and pickled onions,
gorgonzola cheese and salt and vinegar crisps
with four mugs of strong black bitter coffee.

Then he will spend the evening
leaning forward to welcome parents
and talk to them while breathing heavily,
sighing heavily and blowing thoughtfully.

He will also sellotape a smoked kipper on each
    shoe
and place a bowl of dog food under the desk
next to the unclaimed football kit from last term.

(Sometimes he even has one of his baby's nappies
… full and steaming … in his briefcase,
just next to the pupils' work)

It will be a mercifully short evening
for everyone concerned.

Paul Cookson

Rude RIPs

Here lies the body
Of Colin Cole:
Did something rude
With a sausage roll.

R I P

Here lies the body
Of Chrissie Crew.
She died from eating
Cowpat stew.

Here lies the body
Of Bernard Brake.
He ate some dog poop
Which he thought was cake.

John Kitching

Message on the Table

Your dinner is in the
Oven because I'm taking
Uncle
Jack
Up to your grandmother's.
She hasn't seen him in years.
There's also extra sauce in
A pan on the stove. It needs
To be warmed through
Even if you manage to get in on time
Wash up and
Open a can of something extra if you're still
Really hungry, although you
May not be if you work out my
Secret.

David Kitchen

My Take Away was Taken Away

My lizards like their food alive
they want it fresh and kicking
then all those chomps and clicks and
whirrs get chomped by lizard licking.

You buy them in some plastic tubs
just like a take away
then wrap a stack in a carrier bag
go home without delay

The lizard grin was looking thin
last week, I knew that I
must find the pet shop in the town
and buy a fresh supply

I got my box of locust flocks
and started walking back
but popped inside a sandwich shop
for a tasty lunchtime snack

I put the bag beside my foot
started queuing when
I got shoved down by some big bloke
just guess what happened then

My bag with all my lizard food
was stolen in a hurry
by some sad thief who thought he'd nicked
five tubs of top class curry

I don't suppose he realized
until it was too late
it wasn't lamb Madras and rice
leaping from his plate

A buzzing cloud of legs and wings
must have smacked his face
and down his shirt and in his hair
vanished without trace

And locusts being what they are
a population boom
soon will fill this poor man's house
a swarm in every room

I think it served him right you know
for playing such a trick
all those wings and hopping things
I hope they make him sick.

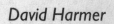

David Harmer

The Yucky Bits Stuck in the Sink

Of all the sights in all the world,
the one that's worst, I think.
is, when you've done the washing up,
spotting the yucky bits stuck in the sink.

The water steams, the bowl just seems
big as a skating rink,
but worst of all is what comes last:
finding the yucky bits stuck in the sink.

The taps go splash, the pots and pans
go crash, and glass goes clink –
until it's time: your hand must go
hunting the yucky bits stuck in the sink.

I find I soon feel rather faint;
my normal "in the pink"
is turning green; I feel quite ill,
feeling the yucky bits stuck in the sink.

Now I can hoover, I can dust,
don't mind the dustbin's stink,
but the task I cannot stick is
fishing for yucky bits stuck in the sink.

Gooey bits and chewy bits, down
the plates I see them slink.
The mucky water drains away,
leaving the yucky bits stuck in the sink.

I face it bravely, stand up tall,
don't close my eyes or blink,
although, no joke, my toes curl up,
poking the yucky bits stuck in the sink.

Pots put away, I go to bed
and sip one final drink,
knowing that, as I sleep, I'll be
dreaming of yucky bits stuck in the sink.

David Horner

Horrible

I was starving.
All I had for breakfast was
one apple and fifteen raisins.
It was half past twelve
and I had to get to Hemel Hempstead.
So I bought a pizza
and I ran and ran
and jumped on my train.

As we pulled out of Euston Station
I began to eat.
Trouble was:
my pizza was in a paper bag –
one
sloppy
cheesey
pizza
with the melting cheese and tomato
stuck
to the bag.

So I peeled the paper off my pizza
but it was all slippery and sticky
and the pizza came off in
soggy lumps
that I scooped together
and pushed into my mouth

blob
by
blob.

But there were dollops of pizza
hiding in the corner of the bag
so I was holding the bag up to my face
tipping it into my mouth
I was drinking pizza
and my fingers were running with
dribbles of tomato
and slops of spicy cheese
all over my knuckles.

So there I was licking at my skin
but my fingers were trailing all over my chin.
So off went my tongue round my face
hunting for drips of pizza
but a bit of paper bag
had got into my mouth
so I was in there trying to get it out
with the finger I was licking.
It was diving into the
slobber
in my mouth
and I was snuffling with my nose
like I was
breathing in
pizza.

It was then
I noticed
the woman opposite.
She was watching me.
She looked like
she had never seen anything
quite
so horrible
in all her life.

Michael Rosen

Earwax, Bogeys and Belly-Button Fluff

Not Quite

He said, "What lovely earrings –
Long and golden brown."
"No," she said, "it's earwax,
Set solid hanging down…"

Clive Webster

Unusual Taste

I'm saving all my dandruff,
every little speck.
The constant shower that settles
from throat right round to neck.

I so wish our school jumper
wasn't navy blue
for every day my shoulders
provide a leading clue

that my scalp is a snowstorm,
a flaking territory,
which makes the cruel jokers
point and laugh at me.

My dandruff's in a jam jar.
I've screwed the lid on tight,
this private, bitter secret –
a growing mound of white.

So next time that school dinner
is spag bol in a pile,
the grated cheese on top will
be something much more vile.

And those who shouted "Scaley",
and made me feel so low,
will eat up all my dandruff.
What's more, they'll never know.

Stewart Henderson

Belly-Button Fluff

"Clean that belly button out,"
William's harassed mum would shout.
"Your belly button's bunged with fluff,"
she'd yell. "It isn't good enough."
Once, William, with a nasty grin
idly poked a peanut in
which settled into all the muck.
Quite forgotten, there it stuck
until the day it grew a sprout.
William couldn't get it out.
He howled and wept, his mother shrieked,
the peanut grew. Within a week
it shot out many leaves and shoots
and in the belly button, roots
twined here and there. Of course, at school
William felt a proper fool.
But he had not long to wait,
the doctors had to operate
and now no boy could be as keen
to keep his belly button clean.

Marian Swinger

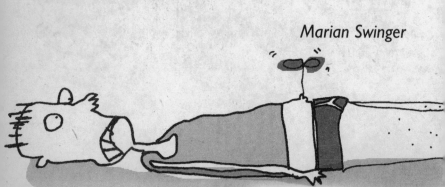

Dad's Hanky

At first sight
Of Dad's hanky
You'll think it has a nice pattern
A nice spotty-green.

But at second sight.
You'll see dad's bogeys take flight.
To add to the hanky's pattern.

Jack Beard (aged 10)

The Scab
(for Jess, Lockie and Jo)

I've never seen one like it.
I'd have you understand
The scab on Daddy's poorly leg
Was bigger than my hand.

Gargantuan, humungous,
A mighty king-sized slab,
And, if you didn't get a look,
You haven't seen a scab.

Children showed him knee-scabs
But they could not compete.
One glance at Dad's monstrosity
And they'd admit defeat.

Grown men begged to see it.
They gasped and turned quite pale
And needed something strong to drink
Before they told the tale.

The scab became as famous
As any scab could get.
Everywhere he went they asked him
Has it come off yet?

That scab it proved a stayer.
The twenty-second day
It loosened at the edges, then
Last night it came away.

No blood and nothing nasty.
It's healed. And all that Dad
Has got to show is dark pink skin.
He's looking rather sad.

Wendy Cope

What Class 4 Fear the Most

We wish our teacher
Would not push
His pencil in his ear.

Not the sharp bit
But the blunt bit
It's the moment we all fear.

He wiggles it
He jiggles it
Turns it round and round.

Then pulls it out
With a squidgy slurp
Looks at what he's found.

Sometimes it's runny
Like golden honey
Dripping on his tie.

Or brown as coffee
Like sticky toffee
Crusty as a pie.

First he sniffs it
Then he licks it
Wipes it on his sleeve.

Then uses it
To mark our sums
Makes our stomach heave.

David Harmer

Wonder Wax

Earwax is so wonderful,
Smooth and toffee gold,
Roll it in your fingers
Then leave it to grow cold
Collect it from your neighbours,
Press it into tins,
Label it organic
Then feed it to the twins.
Use it on the furniture,
Polish your new sandals,
Start a new designer craze,
Give earwax Christmas candles.

Daphne Kitching

A Nose for These Things

An ingenious geezer from Utah
Liked to push mushy peas up his hootah.
    He'd then sneeze a great sneeze,
    Thus releasing the peas,
Giving him quite a deadly pea-shootah!

Graham Denton

The Traffic Light Pick

The traffic light pick
The traffic light pick
You can do it slow
You can do it quick
Slickety slickety slickety slick
Flickety flickety flickety flick

Red! Stop! Handbrake on
You'll be there for days
Here's something everyone
Does to pass the time away.
Male or female, young or old,
Doesn't matter who you are
You think nobody sees you
When you do it in your car.
Get that finger ready for probing and exploring
Get that finger ready for what your nose is
      storing

Fold it, mould it, roll it and bowl it.
Pick it, lick it, flick it and stick it.
Sneeze it, wheeze it, seize it and squeeze it.
Peel it, feel it, don't conceal it.
See it dangle, see it linger on the end of your
      finger
See it swinging to and fro slow in the glow of the
      green for go

Oh no! What to do!
The lights have turned to green.
It's stuck to me like superglue
How do I get my fingers clean?
Where do I stick it? On the wheel.
Where do I stick it? Under the seat.
Where do I stick it? In the ashtray.
Where do I stick it? On my feet.
Where do I stick it? Down my trousers.
Where do I stick it? Over my clothes.
Where do I stick it? On the window.
Where do I stick it? Back up my nose!

The traffic light pick
The traffic light pick
You can do it slow
You can do it quick
Slickety slickety slickety slick
Flickety flickety flickety flick
Yuk!

Paul Cookson

Mucus Memories

I had a vintage bogey
It was the best there's ever been
For beneath its brown crustaceous shell
Lay a core of snotty green.

I wrapped it in some tissue,
And stored it safe with care
In the pocket of my school shorts
So no one found it there.

I would bring it out at playtime
Gathering gangs around the fence
I shocked the girls, impressed the boys
By what my nostril had dispensed.

But my bogey's days were numbered
As it shrivelled in its shroud
And I knew this aging, khaki ball
Could not now draw a crowd.

As I gazed upon my old friend
My teacher wandered by
She squinted at my tissue
And gave a heartfelt sigh

"Oh sultanas, they're my favourite!"
So I cried "Go ahead!"
Then she plucked and sucked and savoured it...
"EXQUISITE TASTE!" she said.

Kate Saunders

Wind Section

A Sports Teacher from Milton Keynes

A sports teacher from Milton Keynes
Had a taste for curried baked beans
Quite often he'd blast
Pupils all looked aghast
As his tracksuits exploded and steamed.

Paul Cookson

That Sound?

What is that strange, trumpeting sound that I hear?
Did it come, as it seemed, from Grandad's rear?
"No, no!" says Grandad. "It was not I.
I tell the truth I do not lie."

But the front room reeks
With pongy fog.
"Aha!" says Grandad.
"It was the dog!"

John Kitching

Shockwave

Carter doesn't trump by half, 'cause wouldn't show up on a seismograph!

Mike Johnson

Bath Time is Laugh Time

The one thing guaranteed to make
Me and my brother laugh
Each night, before we go to bed
Is bubbles in the bath

Mum says, "What's so hilarious?"
But we never, ever tell.
It's bubbles in the bath
And the rather whiffy smell.

We play at ducks – and submarines
Squidge the soap into the hall
But making bubbles in the bath
We like the best of all
Blublublublublublublublu
That's the best of all.

Roger Stevens

Blowing Your Own Trumpet

Little ones, big ones
Snorting like a pig ones
Short ones, long ones
Smelly welly strong ones
Deadly silent ones
Loud and violent ones

Eggy ones, runny ones
Musical and funny ones
Bubble in the bath ones
Those that make you laugh ones
Careful what you do ones
Nearly follow through ones
Those you have to push ones
Careful not to rush ones
Those that make you blush ones

Wet ones, dry ones
Low ones, high ones
Tears in your eye ones

Fast ones, sloooowwww ones
Five rooms in one go ones
Little squeaky mum ones
Machine gun bum ones
Squashy ones, squelchy ones
Big beefy belchy ones

Rhythmic beaty ones
Mighty, meaty ones
Central heated ones

Rusty hinge door ones
Bounce across the floor ones
Gushy mushy peas ones
Those you have to squeeze ones
Those that shake your knees ones
Brussels sprouts and beans ones
Total quarantine ones
Make your trousers steam ones

Morning – after – curry ones ...
To the toilet hurry ones
Surprising and unplanned ones
Just like a brass band ones

Going ... down ... balloooooon ... ones
Blast off to the moon ones
Double trouble trembly ones
Middle of assembly ones
Environment unfriendly ones
Foghorn warning ones
Global warming ones

parp!

flurp!

Icky ones, sticky ones
Got lost in your knicker ones
Whirlwind up your skirt ones
Cyclone in your shirt ones
Every type of noise ones
Girls ones and boys ones…

There's no chance, there's no stopping
The flurp and the parp of fizzy whizz popping
All these noises, everyone's got 'em
'Cause everybody has a musical bottom.

Paul Cookson

When Little Billy Burped

When little Billy burped
it rang out like ten bells
with complicated sound effects
and complicated smells.

Some of it was cottage pie
a lot of it was cheese
with a little splash of cabbage
and quite a lot of peas.

With garlic, beans and onions
mixed up in a hurry
a real whiff of fish and chips
a giant wave of curry.

It swirled around our heads
our faces pale and grey
when little Billy burped
and we got in the way.

David Harmer

—Burp

Storm Warning

"This is an urgent message from your headmistress.
The regional forecast for Oakfield Primary is
    unsettled owing to
A cauliflower shower and chilli front in the dining
    hall.

You can expect a warm southwesterly wind from
    Janie Judd's direction
While occasional bursts of hot air will be felt
    from the book corner.
Light breezes will gently blow from Reception
    Class into the Main Hall
Where there is a chance of a localized tornado as
Billy Smith is doing PE this afternoon
(Cook gave him Double Helpings!)

The wind should be moderate near the girls'
    cloakroom
But getting stronger moving north to the boys'
    loos
Where gusts of over five miles an hour are being
    predicted.
We do advise you to steer clear of this area if an
    alternative route is available
As conditions are already being reported as
    hazardous.

Mrs Hall is hopeful that by story time the
    outlook will be more settled
But there may be some sporadic claps of thunder
    going right on into the evening.

It is likely that this weather pattern will continue
    for several days
As cook has just informed me that baked beans
    and Brussels sprouts
Are on the menu tomorrow."

Kate Saunders

Mr Harding – Silent Assassin

We know he does it
but we just can't prove it.

We can tell by the look on his face,
the glint in his eye and half-formed evil smile.

We know it's him, we just know
but we can never quite catch him.

What happens is this …
just where he has been all mayhem breaks loose.

Coughing, spluttering, the waving of arms
and the pulling up of jumpers over noses.

And it's always one of the lads who gets the
        blame, always.
Last time it was Stewart, he didn't half go red.

We know it's sir, but we can't prove it.
It's not the sort of thing a teacher is supposed to do.

We can't tell the Head – what would we say?
Would they believe us anyway?

How does he do it?

Mr Harding.
Silent but Deadly.

Paul Cookson

Truly Disgusting

Disgusting Love Poem

They went to kiss
But gently missed
Just bad luck I suppose

His mouth too high
The reason why
His tongue went up her nose

Paul Cookson

Love (at Worst Sight)

That's a lovely boil you've got.
What a sight you are.
Can I hold your slimy hand?
Stroke your greasy hair?

Your eyes are so polluted.
Your lips are like two slugs.
Your tongue is long and furry.
Your nostrils full of bugs.

You're the creature I have dreamed of.
I hope you like me too.
I adore that charming scent you wear.
(You pong like a public loo).

Yes, I love the loathsome sight I see.
You're my idea of beauty.
Now, be honest, spit it out,
What do you think of me?

Too clean-cut?
How dare you!

Bernard Young

Run Away! Not Today!

When your teachers lean over you
you want to hold your nose
smelly armpits and smelly breath
you want to run away.

When your parents kiss you
you want to get away
all your friends laughing
you say "Mum, not today".

Rebecca McNeal (aged 9)

The Hairy Kiss

Have you had the hairy kiss?
One from Gran is one to miss!
If she asks you to embrace,
You'd better try and leave the place.

And if you really want,
To avoid her red lipstick,
You can always say,
"I'm really feeling sick."

But if you find you need to,
Stay away from her great moustache,
You could always say,
"Sorry Gran I really need to dash!"

John Baird (aged 9)

Cinema Poem

I like it when
They get shot in the head
And there's blood on the pillow
And blood on the bed

And it's good when
They get stabbed in the eye
And they scream and they take
A long time to die

And it all spurts out
All over the floor
And the audience shivers
And shouts for more

But I don't like it when they kiss.

Roger McGough

Look Who's Talking

You are the dog poo on my shoe!
You are the smell of unwashed socks!
You are the sound of throwing-up!
You are the itch of chickenpox!
You have the IQ of a flea!
You have the manners of a hog!
You are as mouldy as old cheese!
You are as slimy as a frog!
You are much uglier than me!!
Gotcha! It simply isn't true!
That's why we're called identical
I am no uglier than you!

Lindsay MacRae

Yoo-Hoo Sweetheart Give Your Nan a Kiss!

YOO-HOO SWEETHEART GIVE YOUR NAN A KISS!

Nan has come to stay a while
When she tries to kiss me I'll
Grit my teeth and try to smile
There's no chance of that!
There is just one thing I dread,
Lipstick smudges on my head,
I'd rather just shake hands instead ...
There's no chance of that – it's ...

YOO-HOO SWEETHEART GIVE YOUR NAN A KISS!

Then she starts to twist and tweak,
Squeeze the skin upon my cheek,
Does she give me chance to speak?
There's no chance of that!
She won't leave me on my own,
Telling me how much I've grown,
Will I get some time alone?
There's no chance of that – it's ...

YOO-HOO SWEETHEART GIVE YOUR NAN A KISS!

Will she have the pictures
of when I was a tiny tot?
Will she say that I was cute
with my teddy in my cot?
Will she tell my friends
about the first time on my pot?
Then will she embarrass me
with the photos that she's got?
Will she do all this and more
or will she have forgot?
There's no chance of that!

She'll moan about the price of bread,
Tell you who is ill or dead
Then repeat the things she's said,
Moan about the price of bread,
Who is dying, and who is dead,
That much for a loaf of bread?
Ethel died last week she said
Then she'll pat me on the head …

YOO-HOO SWEETHEART GIVE YOUR NANA KISS!

The Relic!

I did it, miss.
Honest, miss.
I spent ages on it – and then, miss.
I was dis – um – stracted, miss.

It was the telly programme you said to see,
    "What the Romans Done for Us",
Only for a moment it was, miss.
About Roman ruins, it was, miss.
And my baby sister grabbed it off the table and, miss,
she was sick, miss
all over my work, miss.

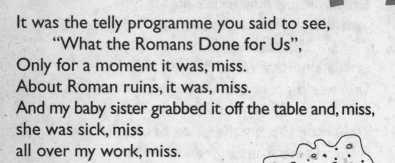

There it was, miss
my drawing of a Roman Auxiliary, taken from that
    picture by Ronald Embleton,
you know the one, miss,
it was covered in all these noodles
and little bits of carrot.

So I washed it, miss,
under the tap, miss.
Then I ran for the bus, still clutching it in my
    hand, miss.

I just made it and stood there
with smelly water dripping on the floor,
And this old bloke, miss.
With a funny blue vein throbbing on his big red
        nose suddenly sniffed, miss.
"Wassat stink?" he says, looking at me.
Well, I didn't know what to do, miss.
So I hung my picture out of the window
        of the bus, miss,
so that the smell might wear off, miss.

And when we stopped at the lights, miss,
you know, the ones by that place,
you know, the hospital place where
        those nurses are, miss.
A 'normous dog jumped up and grabbed
my picture.

So I gets off at the next stop and chases the dog
        down the road, miss.
And before he managed to eat it all I got this bit
        back, miss.
Now if you want, miss,
I'll follow him round with a bucket and a sieve
        for a few days
and get the rest of it back
but otherwise, miss,
I've just got this – it's some Roman remains.

Eric Petrie

Yyyyyyeeeeeuccck!

This will be a filthy one,
a niffy one, a whiffy one,
full of fungus, grot and grime,
poisonous with rot and slime.
    A gungy one, a slummy one,
    a grungy, scummy, crummy one.

It's going to be a greasy one,
a make-you-feel-quite-queasy one.
It crawls with nits, it's soaked in stains,
it's packed with bits folk stuff down drains.
    No scent of roses, more of toes-es.
    (Please place a peg on all your noses.)

A manky, muddy, cruddy one,
a smell far stronger than plain pong,
it's alive with fleas and flies,
and stinks as high as five pigsties!
    An iffy one, a squalid one,
    a squiffy, truly horrid one.

A mangy one, a grebby one,
a dingy and cobwebby one.
A monument to mire and mess,
a masterpiece of muckiness.
    Unkempt, unswept, unwashed, unclean –
    you'd rather not know where it's been.

Yes, it's a mucky stinkeroo,
it's ucky, yucky, icky-poo.
But you couldn't call it crude.
There's nothing naughty, nothing rude.
  Completely off is what it's gone,
  and turned into a dirty one,

not nice at all, and is, I bet,
by far my filthiest poem yet.
Rancid, rank, revolting, rotten,
filled with things best left forgotten.
  But then, when all is said and done,
  it's only words with nothing on.

David Horner

The Sight of Parents Kissing is Very Well Worth Missing

Do you have to do that?
You're not teenagers after all.
You're blocking up the hall
or else sprawled
on the sofa.
Frankly I don't think it's on
for people with three children
to go on kissing for so long.
It's wrong!
And you look nothing like
a pair of fluffy bunnies to me.
She might be your "sweety-darling"
but she's also "Mum".
Put her down please!
We know where she's been
– hoovering under the beds
and unblocking the loo –
How can you still fancy someone
who
does the kind of stuff that she has to do?
You've made her all red in the face
and she's made you
all gooey-eyed.
Parents shouldn't act like this
in fact no one should
who's over twenty-two.

Lindsay MacRae

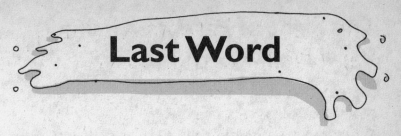

Last Word

My Ten Favourite Disgusting Words*

1.
2.
3.
4.
5.
6.
7.
8.
9.
10.

* Editor's note: I am afraid that the publishers of this book have requested that we do not print the items on this list as they are too disgusting and contravene the Disgusting Things In Print Act of 1787

Roger Stevens

Acknowledgements

The compiler and publishers would like to thank the following for permission to use copyright material in this collection. The publishers have made every effort to contact the copyright holders but there are a few cases where it has not been possible to do so. We would be grateful to hear from anyone who can enable us to contact them so that the omission can be corrected at the first opportunity.

John Baird for "The Hairy Kiss".
Jack Beard for "Dad's Hanky".
Clare Bevan for "Gran's Big Bloomers".
Tony Bradman for "Ten Things to do with a Dead Hamster" © Tony Bradman from Very Silly Lists, pub. Puffin, 2000.
Paul Bright for "How Long Have You Worn Those Pants?".
Liz Brownlee for "Head Lice".
Barry Buckingham for "Question".
Ivor Cheek for "Disgusting Books to Read on the Loo".
John Clarke for "Advice to Anyone Cooped Up in a Hot Car on a Long Journey".
Jane Clarke for "I Wish I was a Kitten".
John Coldwell for "Bite at a Blister" and "My Week was Pants".
Andrew Collett for "Underneath Dad's Armchair".
Paul Cookson for "Lucinda's Sick in the Sink", "Mr O'Donnell's Parents' Evening Plan", "Disgusting Love Poem", "A Sports Teacher From Milton Keynes", "Mr Harding – Silent Assassin", The Last Recorder No One Wants to Play", "Yoo Hoo Sweetheart! Give Your Nan a Kiss!", "Going One Better" © Paul Cookson from Nothing Tastes Quite Like a Gerbil, pub. Macmillan, 1998 and "The Traffic Light Pick" from Big Red Undies, pub. Twist in the Tale, 1996.

Wendy Cope for "The Scab".

Ian Corns for "Dear Teacher".

Karen Costello-McFeat for "After the Party".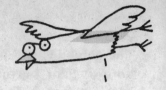

Jan Dean for "Babies Don't Care".

Graham Denton for "A Nose for These Things".

John C. Desmond for "Tush, Tush!".

Gina Douthwaite for "Growth or Moan" and "Sick".

Eric Finney for "Deep Pile" and "Snug as a Bug".

John Foster for "Gran's Dog".

Dez Gusting for "(Bad) Taster".

David Harmer for "Accidents at Teatime", "My Take Away was Taken Away", "What Class 4 Fear the Most" and "When Little Billy Burped".

Stewart Henderson for "Unusual Taste".

David Horner for "Yyyyyyeeeeeuccck!", "The Dung Beetle's Song" and "The Yucky Bits Stuck in the Sink".

Mike Johnson for "Pimple Potion Number Nine" and "Shockwave".

David Kitchen for "Message on the Table" and "Little Jack Horner".

John Kitching for "Our Dog", "Rude RIPs" and "That Sound?".

Daphne Kitching for "Wonder Wax".

Patricia Leighton for "Oo-Phew!".

Lindsay MacRae for "The Sight of Parents Kissing is Very Well Worth Missing" and "Look Who's Talking" © Lindsey MacRae from How to Avoid Kissing Your Parents in Public, pub. Puffin, 2000.

Roger McGough for "Bottom" © Roger McGough from Pillow Talk, pub. Viking, 1990 and "Cinema Poem" from Sky in the Pie, pub. Viking, 1983. Reprinted by permission of PFD on behalf of Roger McGough.

Rebecca McNeal for "Run Away! Not Today!".

Trevor Millum for "Whose Verse is it Anyway?".

Gareth Owen for "Breakfast".

Brian Patten for "The Day I Got my Finger Stuck Up my Nose" © Brian Patten from *Juggling with Gerbils*, pub. Puffin, 2000.

Eric Petrie for "The Relic!".

Daniel Phelps for "Diary of a Toilet Seat".

Scott Richards for "My Class do Revolting Things at the Dinner Table".

Michael Rosen for "Horrible" © Michael Rosen from *The Hypnotiser*, pub. André Deutsch Ltd, 1988 and "Shut Your Mouth When You're Eating" from *Quick, Let's Get Out of Here*, pub. André Deutsch Ltd, 1983.

Coral Rumble for "Grandad's Pants".

Kate Saunders for "Mucus Memories" and "Storm Warning".

Ted Scheu for "Art Museum".

Fred Sedgwick for "A Disgusting Poem".

Roger Stevens for "Bath Time is Laugh Time", "My Ten Favourite Disgusting Words" and "Toe Sucker".

Marian Swinger for "Belly-Button Fluff".

Steve Turner for "The Day I Fell Down the Toilet" © Steve Turner from *The Day I Fell Down the Toilet and Other Poems* pub. Lion, 1996. Used with permission of Lion Hudson.

Lisa Watkinson for "Food".

Clive Webster for "Not Quite", "Party Trick" and "Pretty Parents".

Kate Williams for "Nickie's Knickers".

Bernard Young for "Love (at Worst Sight)".